Isabel Winnifred Donnollan was born in Rockhampton, Australia in 1918, the eldest of Albert and Sarah Hall's 14 children. Isabel became a teacher at 19, married at 23 and raised four children. Isabel, at 36 was elected the First Woman Alderman to Rockhampton City Council and fought for the rights of women teachers.

This book is dedicated to Isabel's children, daughters Rosemary, Elaine and Felicity and to her dear son Timothy who was taken from us too soon.

Isabel Donnollan

WHEN WE
WERE VERY RICH

Cover illustration and all watercolour artwork by

Felicity Prazak

This is a story of when we were very rich – rich in nature, rich in freedom and most of all rich in our family togetherness.

AUSTIN MACAULEY
PUBLISHERS LTD.

A CIP catalogue record for this title is available from the British Library.

ISBN 9781786937292 (Paperback)
ISBN 9781786937308 (E-Book)
www.austinmacauley.com

First Published (2017)
Austin Macauley Publishers Ltd.
25 Canada Square
Canary Wharf
London
E14 5LQ

To Isabel's parents Albert and Sarah Hall and to all her siblings, who shared this unique family life. Joseph (Joe), Albert (Ab), Eileen (Bub), Hazel (Hazy), Cyril (and Daphne who died at birth), Noel, William (Bill), Lenard (Len), Marie and Philomene (Phil) the twins, John, Marguerite (Margie) and Carmel.

Isabel aged 19

Just as the memories of our childhood are nostalgic and coloured by the innocence and the cunning of childhood, so these memories of people are nostalgic, heightened in retrospect, and perhaps more imaginative than true. The people were real, but my memories may be out of perspective; what I believed as a child to be a fact might not have been so. What I, as a child, found insignificant or did not perceive, might have been intensely significant; what I remember as having been said or having happened, may or may not have occurred. My memory has stored them, but my memory may have played me false at times.

How often do we remember back to the sharp impressions of childhood, to find on going back to old scenes, how our memory has enhanced everything? Things tall are now small, things far away are now too near. The eye telescopes what memory has expanded.

CONTENTS

PROLOGUE   17
  ANCESTRY

CHAPTER 1   25
  MILMAN

CHAPTER 2   35
  YAAMBA AND GLENMORE

CHAPTER 3   41
  LIVING AT POWELLL'S

CHAPTER 4   47
  SHOPPING

CHAPTER 5   55
  TRIPS TO THE BEACH

CHAPTER 6   61
  OUR KIND NEIGHBOURS

CHAPTER 7   69
  SCHOOL

CHAPTER 8   81
  TRIPS TO TOWN WITH DAD

CHAPTER 9   95
  KAWANA

CHAPTER 10   103
  OUR NATURAL PLAYGROUND

CHAPTER 11   111
  SNAKES AND VAGARIES OF NATURE

CHAPTER 12   121

  HOME ENTERTAINMENT

CHAPTER 13   127

  READING AND INSPIRATION

CHAPTER 14   135

  A CHANGE OF RELIGION

EPILOGUE   157

PROLOGUE

ANCESTRY

My name is Isabel. I am the eldest daughter of Sarah (Heritage) Hall and Albert Hall.

Our story begins back in 1814, when my Great grandfather Francis Heritage was born near Warwick in England. What troubles young Francis got up to in his early life is not fully documented, but safe to say, in March 1837, aged 23 he was found guilty of burglary and sentenced to seven years imprisonment. He was aboard hulks for nine months in England and then transported to Australia.

Francis sailed from England on the "Moffatt 2" in 1837. It took 137 days to sail, via the Cape of Good Hope, to reach Australia. Francis and 397 other male convicts landed at Hobart in April 1838. Francis was put to work at Patterson's Plains and at the end of 1841 he was recommended for a Conditional Pardon, which he received the following year.

My Great grandmother was Mary Smith. Mary was born in 1818 in England. It seems Mary was in lodgings in Coventry, England when a fellow lodger Elizabeth Baker went out for the day. Elizabeth left behind a cotton gown, two chemises, and apron and a skirt. When Elizabeth returned her clothes were gone. Mary was apprehended nearby, the clothes were found at a pawnshop and the owner remembered Mary bringing them in and the pawnbroker had lent her two shillings on the clothes.

Mary was sentenced to seven years transportation and sailed from London in 1844 on the convict ship "Tasmania". In 1846 Mary had become a "pass holder". A pass holder was in the second last stage of detention and could work in private service for wages.

Mary and Francis were married in the Church of England in Evandale on 6th April 1846. Mary was granted her "free certificate" in May 1851. Several years later, and three children, they sailed to the mainland. They were passengers, along with three children, on board the "Vixen" in January 1852.

This was the time of gold discovery so the family moved around a lot in search of their good fortune. Their seventh child George was born in 1858. George was my Grandfather. Francis and Mary managed to buy some land and settled in Mia Mia Creek, Victoria. Francis had worked with horses in England and worked as a draught horseman, working with the railway companies as the railway lines were constructed around the country. His sons learnt to work with horses, which would be where my grandfather George learned his trade.

George went in search of his own fortune when gold was discovered in Queensland. He met his wife Katherine O'Shea, an Irish girl, in Mt. Morgan, Queensland. They were married on 18th August, 1885 in Blackall, Queensland. They had seven children, Rose, George, Kate, Lily, Eileen, Sarah and Angela. My mother Sarah Hannah Heritage was born on 4th September 1896.

My grandmother, Kathrine O'Shea was born in Rospeth, County Kerry, Ireland. I do not know when she arrived in Australia.

Figure 1 Katherine Heritage (nee O'Shea) – Isabel's maternal grandmother.

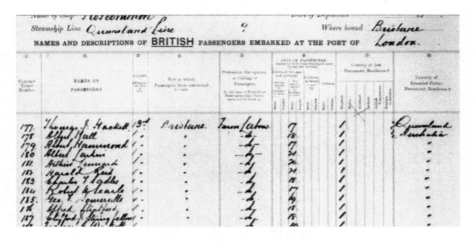

Figure 2 Passenger list of "Roscommon" with passenger Albert Hall

My father Albert Hall was born on 4th July 1893 in South Kensington, London, he was the second youngest son of Benjamin Hall and Catherine Burr.

Albert was 18 years old when he left London on the ship "Roscommon" for Australia on a Church of England youth settlement scheme. We have a copy of the manifest of the "Roscommon", which lists him on the passenger list. He arrived in Australia in 1912. He was an indentured apprentice and worked 3 or 4 years working his passage off at a farm in Toowoomba.

My father was a handsome lad, not tall, with brown eyes and fine dark curly hair. He also had a very mathematical brain and could do all sorts of sums in his head in a flash. However, he was drawn to the bushman's life and developed, from scratch, many of the pioneer's skills with land, cattle and farming. He came from the heart of London. He had lived in Chelsea and often talked of playing in Battersea Park. At one stage he sat for some examination in which he came third in the City of London. He was always very proud of this achievement.

Figure 3 Catherine Hall (nee Burr) – Isabel's paternal grandmother

His father, Benjamin Joseph Hall, a red headed man, had been foreman of a gas works. His mother, Catherine Hall (nee Burr), came from Belfast.

My father Albert was the third youngest of his family, William and Josie being younger than he. He had nieces and nephews older than himself. His sisters were Rose, Alice, Kate, Lily and Josie and his brothers Joseph and William. William was killed in World War I, aged 20. We have a copy of William's Memorial. Joseph was gassed during World War l, but survived.

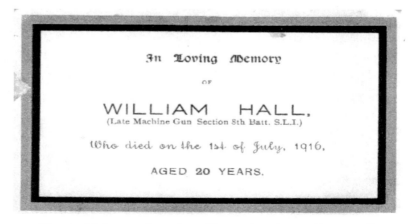

Figure 4 Memorial card to Albert's brother William Hall

20

My mother's father George Heritage came north to Queensland during the gold rushes, seeking his fortune. He drove a bullock team and worked in the early settler's camps where the railways were being laid out west in Queensland. He also worked on the wool wagons, drawn by oxen, which brought the wool into Sydney. He would be away for months. My grandmother Katherine struggled to make ends meet and took in washing, sold fruit and did sewing, but sadly sank into a state of melancholia and had a nervous breakdown. This was when the children were put in the local orphanage. My mother always said that her mother visited the family every month, she became a broken- hearted woman but was unable to take them home again. Sarah, with all but two of her older siblings, had been reared in St. Joseph's orphanage at Neerkol near Rockhampton.

My mother, Sarah, was 3 years old when she went into the Orphanage, her sister Angela was just a baby. The two eldest children Rose and George, escaped the fate of the orphanage because they were too old, by the standards of that time – which meant working aged about 12. The next eldest Kate, Lily, Eileen and Angela were all at the orphanage with my mother.

Mother said that they were always hungry but the orphanage had its own farm so they were able to alleviate this by taking milk direct from the cows, slipping eggs from the fowl house and boiling them in the clothes coppers and roasting potatoes in the ashes of the copper fires. They even used to eat the washing starch! Mother told us of unremitting work at the orphanage, scrubbing the floors and tables, washing, ironing, farm work, baking – they really earned everything they ate! It was my mother's task, at age 9, to bake the bread for all the children in the orphanage.

Sarah left the orphanage at 12 and went into service. Mother said her first wage was one shilling a week for herself and one shilling in the bank. She worked for several families – being young these girls often fell prey to the unscrupulous employers – this happened to several of her friends, but not my mother "*I always kept my honour*". She said this often and fought hard to protect herself, often pushing the furniture against the door at night. She eventually was employed in the family of a doctor. They turned out to be a very kind family.

It was during this employment for the Doctor that Sarah met Albert. Albert used to drive the milk cart and deliver milk to the home. They "walked out" for almost 3 years and were married January 1918. They made a very handsome couple, Sarah was a beautiful bride with her bridegroom Albert (Bert) standing proudly beside her. Their wedding picture has always had pride of place in any home they lived in.

Common route from
England to Australia
subject to prevailing
winds in the 1840's

ΑΠΑΡΚΤΙΑΣ

NORD 0° NORTE

ORIENS

OOST

NEW HOLLANDE

AUSTRALIAS

TASMANIA SOUTH 180°S

1814 Francis Heritage sailed 1897 MOFFATZ

Chapter 1

MILMAN

Figure 5 Isabel aged 2

After they were married, one of the families they had worked for, the Ryans, let Mother and Father live as caretakers on a farm they owned at Milman, about 30 miles from Rockhampton.

My memories begin at the Milman farm around 1921. A high blocked house, with banana trees brushing the verandas – snakes in the banana trees, the cattle being prodded through the dip, my brothers almost falling in the dip, my brothers and I cutting our fingers in the chaff cutter, getting at the separator and mixing up the parts, the thin streams (one of cream and one of skimmed milk) coming from the separator, the delicious taste of the separated milk with its covering of white foam, the yellow cream and the pale yellow homemade butter.

When we ran short of meat my father would kill a bullock or a calf. We children would watch goggle eyed, the shooting, the stringing up on the gibbet, the gutting and skinning and quartering. The other cattle would paw and bellow frantically at the smell of blood.

There was no refrigeration – what could not be used fresh was salted down and put in brine. We used to prise apart the crystals of course salt. There was a reciprocal agreement with the neighbours over slaughtering, meat was shared so that the supply of fresh and salted beef was evened out.

Milman was basically a German settlement and we often went to visit the German neighbours and Dad tasted the different homemade beers they made and we all ate their national dishes. One place kept turkeys. To a small child they were very frightening.

Then the farm was sold and we had to move. Dad built a shanty a mile or so away, near a creek. He would go away on jobs and Mother would have to manage as best she could. Once while getting water from the creek, the water level was so low and she was so weak that she became stuck in the mud. One of her shoes came off and floated away and she did not dare try to retrieve it. How she wept that day! It was her only pair of shoes.

There was only a camp oven to cook with. This was like a large cast iron casserole dish and had to be set over an open fire. In it could be cooked stews, fried meats and delicious pot roasts. When baking bread or damper, the camp oven had to be set in hot coals and hot ashes raked over it. Not the most convenient of mod cons, especially when the cook was pregnant and the temperature a hundred degrees.

Accidents there were. One brother trod in the still hot ashes and seared his feet. Only my mother's quick wittedness and common sense saved him from serious injury. Once, my brothers, poking sticks into the camp fire, set the hessian interior walls of the hut alight. The water tin was empty. My mother flung the contents of the tea pot on the flames and subdued the fire.

Green ants, centipedes, scorpions were all familiar to us and dangers we knew must be avoided. The green ants, however, were too agile and too cunning for us and often gave us a nip which stung for hours.

Snakes did not confine themselves to the ground. Thin green tree snakes were often to be seen twisting in the branches above us as we played. They were said to be harmless but did not look it with their darting forked tongues.

Carpet snakes were familiar to us also. Quite often one would slip unnoticed into the fowl house and would be revealed by its own greed. The lump in its body caused by the hen it had swallowed made its exit through the wire netting impossible.

Feeling uneasy one day over our constant talk of a little lizard that played with us, Mother found us fondling a brown snake, small but lethal. We wondered if its mother was as aghast as ours because it played with children! Another day, lifting out dirty clothes from the tea chest that held them, Mother forked out a black snake.

The eldest brother, Joe, had a well- developed sense of direction and would often lead us, myself and the next youngest brother Ab (all under 4 years old), on a walkabout through the bush. We seemed to go for miles, but he always led us back to the hut. This was through virgin bush!

One of our favourite visiting spots was a scrub turkey's nest. We would watch the birds scratching and heaping the mulch on a mound, obviously used for many years. Mrs Scrub Turkey would lay her eggs and carefully cover them up, leaving them to be hatched by the warmth of the mulch. My memory is of her paying odd visits to the mound as if she were keeping a watchful eye on it and now and again, rearranging the blanket of humus. We never ever saw the chicks, but one day we would come to the mound and know that the chicks had been hatched. Whether Mother Turkey gathered them up there on the mound, I don't know, but I have a distinct impression of us children meeting up with scrub turkeys together with their chickens.

Scrub turkeys made a fine addition to the menu, which was probably quite sparse at that time. There was our share of meat from the kill, there were hens and eggs, skimmed milk which we got for nothing because it was usually thrown away or fed to the pigs. Staples - flour, sugar, rice and oatmeal had to be purchased from the store in town. We always had oatmeal porridge, which was soaked overnight in a large black cast iron saucepan.

Whatever porridge was left was put into the stew, making it deliciously thick and sturdy.

Sometimes, as a luxury, we would get Uncle Toby's Oats, nuttier and tastier than plain porridge. We loved the picture of the old couple saying "Oh, you darling! The oats are delicious". Either on the Uncle Toby's Oats bags or the calico flour bags were printed patterns of dolls and teddy bears, which our mother made up for us by hand and were cherished as almost our only toys.

Dad made hobbyhorses for us and billy carts from fruit cases for the boys "for bringing in the wood and chips". Of course, they often forgot about the wood.

Once the youngest brother Ab thought he'd go walkabout on his own and promptly got lost. My mother did not lose her head. My father was not expected back for some days. She assembled the other children in the hut, gave me charge of the baby and instructed the eldest boy Joe, in quiet desperate tones, that if she did not return by sundown (if she were lost) he was to go along the path to the farm to our other neighbours, the Shegogs. Fortunately the lost brother Ab, had enough sense to bellow like a bull and we clearly heard this roaring through the trees. Beamed in by the noise, Mother homed straight to my bawling brother and had him out of the thick scrub in no time. In her urgency she passed unnoticing through thorns and bushes and returned with her clothes torn to shreds and skin almost as lacerated. Fortunately, no self- respecting snake or dingo would have stayed within reach of that noise of my lost brother.

This same brother Ab (Albert) also fell head first into a post hole, laboriously dug with crowbar and shovel by our father. This post hole was filled with water and Mother pulled him out half drowned. Applying the law of gravity she swung him round upside down till he disgorged the water. She used this method later, on Hazel who almost drowned in a water hole, and again, when Hazel was choking to death on something caught in her throat, she was swung around upside down until she disgorged what was stuck in her throat.

In those days, at least when Mother could devote some time to the older children, she would often make little goodies for us –lemon curd, small cakes, biscuits and gingerbread men with currant features, lovely yellow stick jaw toffee, which we would mould into frogs and animals and snakes all this with only the camp oven and the black iron saucepans.

The cooking utensils also included a large black cast iron frying pan and a huge black cast iron kettle, which would have to be periodically "de furred" of the hard white lining which accumulated and choked it up. It was later found that a marble left in permanently cleaned and eliminated the job of de furring.

Mother cooked some pumpkin tendrils as greens and they were deliciously tender. Vines we had pumpkins, cucumbers, pie melons, watermelons, rock melons and light delicate Indian creams. It was Mother's habit, wherever we lived, to plant seeds from these vegetables all over the place.

Mother also planted lemon, orange and mandarin trees, grown hopefully from seeds. We learned early to tell which was which by the distinctive scents of the lemon and mandarin leave and the little leaflet at the beginning of each orange leaf. Mother also planted banana and pawpaw trees.

It seems strange that wallaby and kangaroo meat did not figure very prominently on the menu. As meat, they were looked down on by the settlers, though they tried to exterminate them, they were looked on as pests as they broke the fences, ate the germinating crops, the grass and drank water that the cattle would use and trampled down household gardens.

The wallaby meat had a "wild" game taste. This could be removed by sponging it with vinegar and encasing it in pastry. It then tasted rather like lamb. Kangaroo meat was gamier, tougher, and more sinewy. On the only occasion I remember tasting kangaroo tail soup, I found it strong and so repulsive that I couldn't eat it in spite of the hunger which had driven us to consider such a dish. Now, of course, kangaroo tail soup is a delicacy!

Wallabies and kangaroos had some value because of their skins, as did possums and koalas. Every now and then, open season was declared on these animals. We often helped our father set out the looped wire snares, set in the grass beside paths or paddies for the hopping animals and in the trees for the climbing animals. Bait was placed in the snares, bread spread with plum jam laced with cyanide. At least, our father told us it was cyanide,

29

but it could have been something else. I cannot now believe that such a dangerous poison, in such a large tin, would be available. We were warned not to touch, sniff or smell it, even an empty tin. The full tins were put up out of our reach. We could climb, but we never dared touch those tins.

N.B. Later on with our research, we found that one of our mother's Heritage cousins, did in fact die at an early age through eating a jam sandwich laced with cyanide, which was meant for bait.

Dad and the boys would skin the dead animals on the spot and carry the already odorous skins home. The ever watchful crows would dispose of the carcasses. Then, the skins would be scraped and "pegged out". If left, they would curl up and become useless. Whatever else was done to them was done mainly by the sun and the ants. They were then folded up carefully and sent to the merchants where they brought barely sufficient to pay for the bait. The whole skin was sometimes used as a floor mat or thrown, for extra warmth, on a bed.

I think my mother rather privately hated this butchery and would not have asked for the extra animals to be killed. *"I don't like animal skins"* she would say *"they get full of fleas"*. To us children there was no cruelty involved. The animals were already dead when we saw them, and animals dead from natural causes were always to be seen. If the snares acted quickly, the animal died quickly; if they acted slowly, it had time to make its escape.

There were open seasons too, for wild duck which also had a fishy weedy gamey taste. Still, they were food, and again, sponged with vinegar they were palatable. If a wild duck stew were made, a few spoons of vinegar were put in the stock.

Then there were the mushrooms, lovely succulent large as dinner plates. It wasn't always easy to tell them from the other deceptive fungi, but we came to recognise the top from brown to gleaming white, the under- part pink to maroon red, thick stems, the skin easy to peel and the mushroom like smell. Fried in butter or beef dripping in the camp oven or in the black iron frying pan over the open fire, what delicious breakfasts they made. Especially the delectable juices mopped up to the last drop with homemade bread.

We always had them for breakfast because my Dad and I went out in the dewy mornings at the crack of dawn to gather them. The boys were too young and too heedless to be trusted to distinguish between good mushrooms and bad. To me, these were the main ingredients of a mushroom breakfast, first a little girl and her Daddy and the dawn streaked sky.

Once, returning from our neighbours the Shegogs, along the path, we found scattered a number of eggs. To my eye they seemed as large as pullet's eggs. My Daddy gathered up some and we took them home. They were very rubbery and slippery. When they finally hatched, they were found to contain small lizards. Probably those fat short lizards that we met often in the grass. They did nothing but poke out blue tongues and eye us wickedly. If they were poked with a stick, they would thrust forward their heads and advance a threatening inch. We would scuttle to safety, never really believing that these fat sluggish, blue tongued lizards would be able to catch us.

Miraculous escapes we had too. Many was the snake that slithered out of our way as we rushed headlong. Many was the time we "nearly fell into" the creek when getting water.

My father would often take me up before him on his spirited pony, Nip. While visiting Shegogs' one day, he left the pony tied to the fence with me still on its back. Our equally spirited dog came up and nipped at the pony's heels. In a twinkling, I was thrown to the ground, the pony plunging and rearing about me, tied by his head and tormented from behind by the dog. There were several anxious moments while the horse was quieted and untied and someone crept in and whisked me away apparently, none the worse, except for a hoof mark across my stomach and another across the forehead. But it was a long while before I ceased to dream of those thrashing, stamping, metal shod feet and that wild eyed swinging head. For some time after that, I had quite a phobia about horses.

Having been brought up in England and worked as a waiter in a Gentlemen's Club in the heart of London, my father embraced life in Australia, he took on all sorts of jobs to keep his growing family; share farming, milking, ploughing, fencing, picking corn (by hand), horse breaking, dipping cattle and felling timber. His apprenticeship on the farm in Toowoomba had given him good training.

One job with vivid memories for us was tree felling, cutting down trees and breaking them up into sleepers to support railway lines. It was hard dangerous work requiring muscle and skill. An indentation would be chopped on the side opposite to the way the tree was to fall, then with one man on each end of the saw, the job of tree felling would begin. The long supple crosscut saw would bite away at the trunk, each man moving in a rhythmic movement till they would stop, judge how much further, saw a little more and then move out of the way. The great tree would stand still in surprise for a moment, then teeter disbelievingly till the remainder of its girth was shredded, then bowing to the inevitable, it would crash resoundingly, bounce a little and then lie still. I always felt sorry for the giant laid low.

Next, the branches would be trimmed off with axe or hand saw and sometimes, the bark removed. Splitting the trunks was tricky. First the direction of the grain had to be ascertained, then wedges were carefully driven in forcing the splits wider, the back of the axe being used as a hammer. It was risky work. The wedges sometimes slipped and fingers, hand or feet could be crushed.

Axes were sharpened on a round grindstone, mounted on a stand and turned by a handle; turning the handle was a job we didn't mind doing. Sparks would fly off the axe head and the bitten edge would firm into a shining silver grey line. My father would test the keenness of the edge on a piece of paper or on the hairs of his arm.

The big saws were sharpened with a file. The boys frequently "borrowed" the saws and left great gaps in the teeth. They could not guess at the exasperation and despair this caused. The saws were greased with unsalted dripping and covered during a storm as there was a belief that they would attract lightning.

We were fortunate that the mishaps that occurred were minor ones, though some carried overtones of tragedy. Our father received a great gash around the base of his thumb, leaving a mark he carried for years. The great worry in those days, with a wound, was "lockjaw".

My brother Joe and I loved taking smoko (morning or afternoon tea) to Dad as he was working. We carried the sandwiches and scones or biscuits in a knotted tea towel and swung a billy of scalding hot black tea between us. The handle was hot and often the billy was more empty than full by the time we arrived.

One such day we rushed full pelt to Dad, where he and another man were felling a large tree. It was just that second when the tree begins to fall and we rushed on unheeding as Dad shouted "*Get back! Get back!*" as they stared at us with horror struck faces.

Everything seemed to be in slow motion as we stood frozen in the path of the tree, finally cognisant of our danger. Father seized his axe and with superhuman strength, gave a mighty blow to the trunk. It shuddered in mid-air, twisted a degree and fell away from us at an off angle. We were enmeshed in the leaves, but unharmed. The slipping base missed Father by a fraction. It would have broken his arm. We got a "good hiding" that day and we were lucky at that.

As the eldest, I have memories the other children do not have. Moonlight nights, walking home from the farm or our neighbours the Shegogs with my Daddy: the mournful curlews overhead; the howling of dingoes; the realisation that sometimes they were a shade too close.

When encountered, the dingoes on the track would slink aside, their empty eyes reflecting the moon fire. The feeling that they were behind you on the track was worse than knowing they were ahead of you. It meant that you were being followed.

Not being accounted daring enough to attack a man, the dingoes were disregarded. Trackers have reported dingo tracks following man tracks when wandering men have been lost or crazed by thirst. There was no telling what would happen if a large strong dingo or pack of dingoes met a solitary man, weary or ill or a trifle "merry" or a small child. One night, as the drought progressed, Dad was bailed up by a hungry and thirsty half crazed dingo. Dad didn't hesitate, and laid into the dingo with a good thick waddy and drove it off.

The lack of rain was about the last straw for my spartan mother. The land was in the grip of drought; the creek had dried up; bush fires threatened; she was pregnant again. Now it seemed that her family was in danger from the dingoes.

Chapter 2

YAAMBA and GLENMORE

After Mother went into town and had baby number four, Eileen, in 1922 we moved into a house on the outskirts of Yaamba, about ten miles away from Milman. The rain came and pink rainlilies bloomed around the steps of the cottage, which was about 4 steps up with 4 rooms and a verandah. The house was overhung by a huge mango tree, whose fruit the landlord reserved to himself. We never picked any of this fruit, but on occasions we did help the wind to shake it down.

My father had to go away to jobs for a fortnight at a time and my mother lived rather in terror of this landlord, who called for the rent each week and abused my shrinking mother if my father was late getting back with the rent.

Life there had its interest for us children. We had never met up with an echidna before. We called it a "porcupine". Warned by our dog's wounded nose, we did not go too near it. Entrenched near the back steps, it burrowed and burrowed and disappeared before our eyes. Another one was coaxed into a corn bag, which was then tied up. Next morning, the echidna was gone leaving a large hole in the bag.

Near the back steps was a large hole into which we were always poking sticks. Into this one day, slithered a beautiful ring snake, coal black with stark white rings. The boys grabbed the snake's tail but our busy barking dog brought mother out to see what all the fuss was about. She soon boxed the ears of two boys fighting over a snake's tail.

Yaamba had been cleared, no bush too close to the settlement. The shops were some distance away, but Mother could keep her eye on me as I trudged along the road. I well remember a day when the butcher's pet sheep chased me. I was terrified of that monster with his huge curled horns. As he

35

advanced, I ran for my life dragging behind me in the dust, the string of sausages for our tea.

I was rescued by a most marvellous kind lady, riding by on a light pony. She was the wife of the local policeman. She took me up before her and deposited me at home, dusty sausages and all. Later she came to see my mother with a parcel of clothes for us. Mine included an embroidered white voile dress with a blue ribbon sash; a tussore silk dress; a knitted sky blue jumper and a white polo necked jumper. I prized these very much.

Across the flat lived a gentle old silver haired dark skinned man, reputed to be an escaped American slave. He always wore a waistcoat with a dangling watch and chain. He was a most gentlemanly old man. One day, while taking us for a walk, my mother lost her wedding ring in the long grass. To try to find it she set fire to a small patch of grass. A wind sprang up and the fire got out of control, threatening the house, which we children had been told not to leave.

Exhausted, pregnant, desperate, Mother was almost fainting into the fire, when the old dark gentleman came to her rescue. The flames were curbed and he helped her poke through the smoking debris until the wedding ring was found. Her skin grazed, face blackened, hair scorched, Mother came home triumphant and promptly collapsed. Other friends, alerted by old Dick, came and bathed her and put her to bed. Thanks to them she did not lose the baby, but the experience seemed to change her for some time.

Not very far away was a river, a tributary of the Fitzroy, with overhanging banks on one side and a smooth sandy beach covered with white pebbles on the other. From the high bank you could gaze down into the depths, see the fallen imprisoned trees and the lurking fish. You could slide down the steep bank and land at the water's edge (if Mother was not close!). Little we worried about the snags that could hold us down forever.

In drier weather, the river could be forded. We often waded across to the sandy stretch. Sand to roll in, to trickle between fingers and toes! White pebbles to skip across the water! Cool water to paddle in. Mother said there were quick sands which would swallow us up if we wandered away.

Sometimes, Dad took us fishing. Kookaburras lined the boughs of the tall white river gums; peewits squabbled overhead; crows cawed inquisitively; the sun shone hotly. We rolled down the grassy banks and skipped stones; disturbing the fish. Surprisingly, amid all this commotion, the catch was good silver perch, yellow bell, barramundi, mullet, catfish and jewfish. I could never understand the aversion some people expressed towards catfish and jewfish. Cooked as Mother did them, in bread crumbs, they were delicious.

One day a letter came. It was from a man Dad had worked for before, offering him a job as a share dairy farmer. My mother wept for joy. .Life at Yaamba for them had been grim. We moved to the dairy farm four miles outside Rockhampton.

Shortly afterwards, their fifth child Hazel was born. They had now been married 7 years and had a family of 2 boys and 3 girls. Prospects now booked brighter. Beside the supply of milk, butter and cream from the dairy, there were eggs, ducks and hens, for the table. Eggs for custards and puddings and cakes. Fried egg, boiled eggs, scrambled eggs, poached eggs, omelettes. Wonderful.

Dad had decided to rear pigs. Just as he, the Londoner, had developed all the bush man's skills, now he made neat pens, did the concreting, rigged up a pump and pipeline to bring water to the pigs.

We lived in a high blocked house, no electricity or town water. The house had bedrooms and a verandah upstairs, downstairs it had a kitchen living room with an incubator recess and a stove recess. The stove was black cast iron. Cleaning and blackening the stove became a regular job.

The floor downstairs was made of bricks set in the earth, the downstairs was walled in with corrugated iron. There were proper water tanks on proper tank stands. The front steps had no railings but the back steps did. Good for sliding down the railings.

We were back in the familiar world of cattle, milking times, separators and chaff. The dear, gentle cows. Their mildly reproachful gaze when we flipped Daisy's tail or tweaked hair from Strawberry'. When we caught a swishing tail across our ears, I'll swear those eyes twinkled wickedly. The darling little new born calves and the frisky poddy ones. They would put their heads down and pretend to butt you. As they are heifers their horns were harmless. The poor little bull calves were not allowed to live long they became table veal or were boiled down for the pigs.

We were fascinated by these grunting squealing pigs and little pink piglets. Roast suckling pig was added to the menu. Somehow we never made the connection between the meat served up at the dinner table and the lively energetic animals we loved.

On the farm the boys rode the horses bareback without fear. I was still dubious about horses and did not try this. When the boys didn't ride the horses, they chased them. With heels flashing and tails floating, the animals enjoyed the chase as much as we did. The dainty little long legged foals joined in the fun.

Besides ducks and hens, there were bantams and guinea fowls. For a while, there were two peacocks which strutted and displayed their beautiful tail feathers. Alas, their days of proud dignity were over. Too often they had to fold tails and take flight with the boys in pursuit.

We had never lived in a dwelling with neighbours on our doorstep and neither had we any close here, but some were in sight. About a quarter of a mile away were half a dozen houses in a row, but we were free to run around, to make as much noise as we liked.

We weren't allowed to swim in the duck pond, but my brothers often fell in accidentally. There was an island, however, in the pond and how could you get to it without getting wet?

We could swim in the pump hole creek and we often did when our father had to repair the sanguinary pump engine, which was often. The pumping end of the creek was quite deep, but the creek leading up to it was shallow. The banks were high and slippery, piled with clay, which Dad had dug out and slung on the bank. Just as well we could only go in while he was there. To slip into the murky muddy water was very frightening. We could not swim at that time and I was hauled out twice.

There weren't many trees in this area, a few scattered gums and brigalow, some sheoaks along the water hole. In the back paddocks were several felled trees. Two of these were very wide in girth and very long. My brothers irreverently named them Mrs Allen and Mrs Hagstrom after two

38

very plump matrons in the district. If we were playing on Mrs Allen, Mum knew just where we were. You could run along the logs for several feet, jump off; then climb through the fallen branches, each as big as a tree itself. The bark had long since stripped away and the trees were blackened in patches from grassfires. Mrs Hagstrom was hollow and sometimes we were fortunate enough to see a goanna or possum there.

We loved the bottle trees, especially if they had been burnt out, hollow trunks for hiding and roots burned into a soft ash a good place to play in. Here we met again the crows, magpies, peewits, butcher birds and swallows nesting in the barn, sparrow hawks hung in the sky, grass birds skittered away from their nests in the long grass, willy wagtails danced cheekily on the cows' backs.

The property was overrun with prickly pear. We liked the fruit but the pear was continuously poisoned in an effort to destroy it. Nothing was any good until the cactoblastis moth was introduced. The flamboyant orange and yellow black cactoblastis caterpillars made short work of the prickly pear.

Prickly pear has two kinds of thorns, great huge pin type thorns on the leaves and clusters of small splintery thorns on the fruit, the fruit was delicious to eat. The juice was bright red and dyed our faces and clothes alike. I can remember my mother making a dye out of it. To prepare the fruit, it was plucked cautiously, then rolled over and over in dirt, sand or grass to remove the thorns, then the thin skin was slivered off and the fruit popped into the mouth. Too bad if all the prickles weren't off!

Chapter 3

LIVING AT POWELLL'S

The sheds and Powell's old house were full of old harness, old lamps and drays. Dad went to town in the sulky with one horse. When the whole family went out, we went in the waggonette with a top – drawn by two horses.

Not far from our kitchen door was a wood heap. Now and again a goanna, with an appetite for hen's eggs was found basking there. Boys and dogs would join in the chase until the old goanna would decide that peace was preferable to food and it would run up a tree. There was no flower garden except a clump of geraniums and the vegetable garden was planted by Mother, mostly melons, tomatoes and pumpkins.

Dad had a regular round of shops, hotels and boarding houses where he collected scraps to feed the pigs. Fruit shops threw out cases and cases of good fruit, the "specks" which the fruit shops now sell unblushingly as "first quality" fruit. Very little of it was really specked and we often had cases with hardly a marked fruit. When there was a glut on the market the prices fell, whole cart loads of cabbages, carrots, onions, potatoes, watermelons, pumpkins, marrow, bunches of bananas, bags of beans would be thrown out, most of them prime quality. Many a meal Mother made for the family from these vegetables.

Mt. Morgan and Rockhampton had hordes of goats and the health men staged raids on them. The cart came home heaped up with slain goats to be boiled down for the pigs. Sometimes they would be sent out live and their throats cut at the farm. The bleating was pitiful. There were baby kids docile, pink and white, sweet as lambs, agile, leaping all over the place. Why did they have to grow into great smelly old goats? We reared a few, but the adult goats demolished so many gardens that they went the way of the rest. After that roast kid was added to the menu.

At times Dad would put a small tank on the cart and it would lumber to the butter factory for buttermilk. Dad would get a big billycan full for us. It was delicious, cold and salty with little globules of butter floating in it. Mother would often make buttermilk scones. As the butter factory also made ice, Dad would get a block to take home and perhaps a handful of crushed pieces for us to suck. How beautiful we thought that ice! Like a flawed diamond, it fascinated us with all its crazes and crevices the colours it reflected the slipperiness, the coldness, the numb fingers and all the while it slowly melted away and we greedily licked the cold droplets Heavenly!

A favourite pastime of the boys was looking for the fowl's nests. The cunning hens and ducks and guinea fowls "laid away". They paraded around innocently looking as if they didn't even know what an egg was. Then one day they would appear with a clutch of little chickens or ducks or guinea chickens and looking so pleased with themselves!

The boys soon woke up to all their hiding places, the old stumps, the bushes, the wait a while vines, the harness room, the old carts, even the wagonette. All the same, the score was even, there was a hidden nest to match each one located. Often the hen was broody, her eggs therefore too advanced to be edible, so hers was a victory.

For the convenience (really inconvenience) of the housewife, the wash bench was set well away from the kitchen door, so that she had to go half way around the building for the washing that had to be done every day. Little was known about baseball here at the time, but the wash bench, boiler, wood heap and clothes lines were set out in a rough diamond shape, so that the housewife was obliged to cover ten times more ground that needful.

Our house occupied the middle of one side of the rectangular shaped flat ground which fronted it. Along the opposite side ran the Four Mile Road with half a dozen houses sitting comfortable on their allotments on the far side of the road. On our side, at the corner of the flat, was the home of Ma Robson. The fourth side of the flat was formed by the back fence of another farmhouse, which fronted the Four Mile Road where it branched at right angles.

On this flat grew many wait a whiles, a climbing plant with clutching tendrils. If you caught your clothes on this, you had to wait quite a while to untangle yourself. The plant had a pretty, faintly scented white flower, which attracted swarms of black and white butterflies. They covered the plants in clouds and could be picked off by holding the wings together with the thumb and forefinger. The plant was host too, to the larvae. Thousands of small creamy eggs were laid on the underside of the leaves and a week later the plants were covered with thousands of black and white caterpillars chewing steadily, then each would turn into a black and white chrysalis. We collected several of these and over and over again watched the damp, struggling butterfly emerge, rest awhile and fly off, a dainty fluttering miracle.

There were other chrysalises, in beautiful iridescent greens, gold, silver and blues, on the trees, vines and grasses. These were highly prized. Usually the colour outside gave an indication of the lovely creature within. The wait a whiles produced a plum shaped fruit popular with children. "Sticky buns" they were called and though we were forbidden to eat them, we did and suffered no ill effects.

After a flash flood, while swimming in the running water, we discovered a very strange creature. *"Come quick Mum, a little alligator"*. The mud blue thing advanced on us, it was a yabbie. We always called it a crawfish or a crawchie. The pump hole, being muddy, provided a plentiful supply of yabbies, which when cooked, taste rather like crab with varying degrees of weediness. The boys became quite expert at picking them up by grabbing the two nippers. To cook them, a saucepan of water was brought to the boil, a handful of salt thrown in, then the live yabbie was dropped in, dying instantly. When cooked, it became a bright red and it was very tasty. The nippers and tails contained the edible flesh.

To catch them you tied some chunks of meat, the smellier the better, to lines of black cotton, then let them down into the muddy water, outside a yabbie's hole, if one could be found in the creek bank. The cotton must not be white because that could be easily seen against the muddy water. When the line quivered we knew that yabbie had hooked his two nippers into the meat. The cotton was drawn up slowly to within about a foot of the surface and a scoop slipped under him. Once the yabbie broke the surface, he would let go and drop back into the water or into the scoop if your judgement was correct. Sometimes an odorous bone suspended on a string was pulled through the water first to whet their appetites and draw them out of their holes. Some yabbies were surprisingly large.

43

The materials used for the scoops caused some heart burning. A pouch of cloth or fine wire netting or mosquito netting, fastened to a ring of fencing wire, extended to form a handle. Mosquito netting wasn't popular with Mum, especially if cut out of a perfectly good net. Nor was I happy about the use of my hat a basin shaped confection of shiny pink and grey straw. To add insult to injury, I wasn't even given a share of that particular catch! The fishermen ate the large yabbies' and bestowed the smaller ones on others as a mark of special favour. As I had put on such a performance about the use or misuse of my hat, my rating was then extremely low.

Stan, a friend of my parents, who had been best man at their wedding, would often call to visit Mother and Father. Stan had a plump pretty wife named Lil, who dressed in the height of fashion. They had three little girls, always in dainty dresses. Stan and Lil often visited us. They had a shiny red Ford. When his funds accumulated my father decided to get a car. It was a buttercup yellow Buick with a canvas hood. We went off to see Stan and Lil. She gave us Kraft cheese sandwiches. We had been used to the hard loaf cheese, Dad's taste inclined to the rather strong types, so we were not over fond of cheese, though we liked the red luncheon cheese in tins. This Kraft cheese was a revelation, in a small packet, soft, easily cut in slices. It blended with the fresh bread and butter well. After that we pestered Mother for Kraft cheese and refused to look at any other.

"NB As a footnote to their friend Stan, when Mother died at age 103 1/2, at her funeral a lady came up to my sister Eileen and spoke to her. Eileen couldn't make out who this lady was at first until the lady told her *"my father Stan was best man at your parent's wedding and we played together when we were little".*

Beside the daily trip for pig food, other trips had often to be made – for grain for the cattle and fowls; for buttermilk; and sometimes, during drought times, to the standpipe for tanks of water; to the market with pigs or fowls for sales. The dray was also needed at various places on the farm, for carting firewood, for delivering eggs to the shops. The horses were getting old, the harness constantly needed repairs. Horses had to be shod, groomed and fed. First they had to be caught and they didn't always have a mind to be caught. New horses had to be broken in.

Dad traded in the Buick and bought a Ford truck. Its number was 66 846. An expensive item for the family but at last Mother could go to town. Dad managed his money but Mother sent us out with our billy carts laden with plums and apples for sale. She sold eggs and homemade butter. A grocer threw out his assortment of out of date seed packets we went around selling these too. This must have been Mother's pocket money. Dad took us to town and occasionally, mostly window shopped, there was not the money to buy children new clothes, we had hand me downs, given by kindly neighbours.

Dad also took us if we ever needed to see the doctor. I had repeated attacks of tonsillitis, so it was decided that my tonsils would have to be taken out. Dad told me that we were in a restaurant and that the nurse was the waitress who took our order. She took me into a room, took off my dress and shoes and put ME on the table. I thought I was going to be eaten up and screamed the place down. I tried to get away, but dozens of hands (it seemed) held me down and a foul smelling mask was held over my face. When I awakened, the operation was over.

As we left the surgery, I kept spitting out blood. My father said that was the medicine I had been given. When we got home my mother gently told me that my tonsils had been taken out. If only they had told me beforehand! I was ill more from shock than from the actual operation.